MUSICAL TERMS
& SIGNS

IN A NUTSHELL

Maureen Cox

This paperback edition published in 2015 by **Mimast Inc**

Copyright © Mimast Inc 2015,

Canadian ISBN 978-1-987926-08-8

All enquiries regarding this electronic edition to:

Mimast Inc
Edmonton
Alberta T6R 2H9
Canada
email: mimast@telus.net

From the sale of this book the Author
and Publishers will make a donation to
The Elizabeth Foundation incorporating
The Beethoven Fund For Deaf Children
(Charity Registration no. 293835).

WORDS & TERMS
in Alphabetical Order

LOOK UP
A TERM

FIND THE MEANING

A

a (à) - at, to, by, for, in the style of

aber - but

accelerando - becoming gradually faster

accent - emphasize, make a particular part more important

adagietto - rather slow

adagio - slow, leisurely

adagissimo - very slow

ad libitum; **ad lib.** - at choice; play freely

affetuoso - tenderly

affrettando - hurrying

agile - swiftly

agitato - agitated

alla - in the style of

> **alla breve** - make your speed twice as fast as you would have done
>
> **alla marcia** - in the style of a march
>
> **alla polacca** - in the style of a polonaise

allargando - broadening out

allegretto - slightly slower than allegro

allegro - lively, reasonably fast

allegro assai - very quick

alto - high; often refers to a voice, higher than a tenor but lower than a soprano

amabile - amiable, pleasant

amore - love

andante - at a walking pace

andantino - a little slower or faster than andante

anima - life, feeling

> **con anima** - with feeling

animato - lively, animated

animé - animated, lively
appassionata - with passion
arco - play with the bow
arioso - airy, melodious
assai - very
assez - enough, sufficiently
attacca - go on immediately
ausdruck - expression
avec - with

B

baritone - voice between bass and tenor
bass - the lowest of the standard four voice ranges,
    soprano, alto, tenor, bass
bellicoso - warlike, aggressive
ben or bene - well
    ben marcato - well marked
bewegt - with movement. agitated
bravura - with boldness and spirit
breit - broad, expansive
brillante - sparkling, brilliant
brio - vigour;
    con brio - with spirit, with vigour

C

calando - getting softer, dying away
calore - warmth
    con calore - warmly
cantabile - in a singing style
cantando - in a singing style
cédez - yield, relax the speed

col - with

come - as

> **come prima** - as before
>
> **come sopra** - as above

comodo - comfortable

> **tempo comodo** – at a moderate speed

con - with

> **con anima** - with deep feeling - soul
>
> **con brio** - with vigour
>
> **con moto** - with movement
>
> **con sordini** - play with a mute
>
> **con spirito** - with spirit, life, energy

crescendo [cresc.] - gradually louder

D

da capo [d.c.] - from the beginning

dal segno [d.s.] - repeat from the sign [𝄋]

decelerando - slowing down; decelerating;

deciso - with determination

decrescendo [decresc.] - gradually softer

delicato - delicately

diminuendo [dim.] - gradually softer

dolce - sweetly

dolcissimo - very sweetly

dolente - sadly

dolore - grief, sorrow

doloroso - sorrowfully, plaintively

doppio - double

doppio movimento - double the speed

douce - sweet

E

e; ed - and
ein - a, one
einfach - simple
ein wenig - a little
empfindung - feeling
encore - again; perform the relevant passage once more
en dehors - prominent
energico - energetic, strong
enfatico - emphatically
en pressant - hurrying forward
en retenant - slowing
espirando - dying away
espressione - expression
> **con gran espressione** - with great expression
> **con molta espressione** - with much expression
espressivo [espress., espr.] - with expression, feeling
estinto - as soft as possible, lifeless
et - and
etwas - somewhat, rather

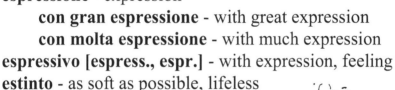

F

facile - easily , without fuss
feroce - ferociously
feurig - fiery
festivamente - cheerfully
fieramente - proudly
fine - the end
> **al fine** - to the end
flebile - mournfully
focoso or fuocoso - fiery, passionately

fortepiano [*fp*] - loud, then immediately soft

forte [*f*] - loud

fortissimo [*ff*] - very loud

forza - force, power

    con forza - with force

forzando [*fz*] - with a strong accent

freddo - cold, unemotional

fresco - freshly

fröhlich - cheerful, joyful

funebre - funeral

    marcia funebre - funeral march, indicating a stately and somewhat plodding tempo.

fuoco - fire

    con fuoco - with fire, in a fiery manner

furia - fury

furioso - furiously

G

gaudioso - with joy

gentile - gently

geschwind - quickly

getragen - sustained

giocoso - merry

giusto - strictly, exactly

    tempo giusto - in strict time

grandioso - in a grand manner

grave - slowly and seriously

grazioso - gracefully

gustoso - with happy emphasis and forcefulness

H

hervortretend - prominent, pronounced

I

immer - always
imperioso - imperiously
impetuoso - impetuously
incalzando - getting quicker
innig - intimately, heartfelt
insistendo - insistently, deliberate
in modo di - in the style of
intimo - intimately
irato - angrily
-issimo - a suffix meaning extremely
    fortissimo - extremely loud
    prestissimo - extremely fast
-issimamente - a suffix meaning as can be
    leggerissimamente - as light as can be

K

kräftig - strongly

L

lacrimoso or lagrimoso - tearfully, sadly
lamentando - lamenting, mournfully
lamentoso - lamenting, mournfully
langsam - slowly
largamente - in a broad style
larghetto - faster than largo
larghezza - broadness
    con larghezza - with broadness; broadly

larghissimo - very slowly; slower than largo

largo - slow & stately, broad

lebhaft - lively

legatissimo - as smoothly as possible

legato - smoothly

légèrement, **leggiermente** or **leggiadro** - lightly,
    delicately

leggierissimo - very lightly and delicately

leggiero - lightly

lent - slowly

lentando - gradual slowing and softer

lentissimo - very slowly

lento - slowly

liberamente - play freely

libero - free, freely

l'istesso, lo stesso - the same

lo stesso tempo or **l'istesso tempo** - the same tempo,
    despite changes of time signature

lontano - from a distance; distantly

lugubre - mournful

lunga - long

> **lunga pausa** - long pause

lusingando: coaxingly

M

ma - but

> **ma non troppo, ma non tanto** - but not too much

maestoso - majestically, in a stately fashion

magico - magically

magnifico - magnificent

main droite - right hand (abbreviation: md or m.d.)

main gauche - left hand (abbreviation: mg or m.g.)

malinconico - melancholic

mais - but

mancando - dying away

mano destra - right hand (abbreviation: md or m.d.)

mano sinistra - left hand (abbreviation: ms or m.s.)

marcatissimo - with much accentuation

marcato, marc. - marked, accented

    ben marcato - well marked

marcia - a march

    alla marcia - in the manner of
        a march

martellato - hammered out

marziale - in a military style,
    solemn and fierce

mässig - at a moderate speed

medesimo tempo - same tempo, despite changes of time
    signature.

melancolico - melancholic

meno - less

    meno mosso - less movement

mesto - sadly

mezzo forte [*mf*] - moderately loud

mezzo piano [*mp*] - moderately soft

mezzo-soprano - voice between alto and soprano

misterioso - mysteriously

misura - measure

alla misura - in strict time

    senza misura - in free time

mit - with

mobile - flexible, changeable

moderato - at a moderate pace

modéré - at a moderate speed

moins - less

molto - very

moto - motion

 con moto - meaning with motion or quickly

morendo - dying away

mosso - movement

moto - motion

movimento - movement

munter - lively

N

nicht - not

niente - "nothing", barely audible, dying away

nobile or nobilimente - in a noble fashion

non - not

 non tanto - not so much

 non troppo - not too much

O

obbligato - required, indispensable

ohne - without

ossia - or

ostinato - obstinate, persistent; refers to a short musical pattern that is repeated throughout an entire composition or portion of a composition

P

parlando - in a speaking manner

parlante - in a speaking manner

pastorale - in a pastoral style, peaceful and simple

patetico - with feeling

pausa - rest

penseroso - thoughtfully, meditatively

peu à peu - little by little
perdendosi - dying away
pesante - heavily
peu - little
a piacere - at pleasure; need not follow the rhythm strictly
piacevole - pleasant, agreeable
piangendo - literally 'crying'
piangevole – plaintive
pianissimo [_pp_] - very soft
piano [_p_] - soft
pietoso – pitiful
più - more
più mosso - more movement
pizzicato [pizz.] - plucked
plus - more
pochettino; poch. - very little
poco - a little

    poco a poco - little by little
    poco più allegro - a little faster
poi - then
    diminuendo poi subito fortissimo - getting softer
        then suddenly very loud
pomposo - pompous, ceremonious
possibile - possible
precipitato - precipitately, hurriedly
presto possibile - as fast as possible
presser - hurry
en pressant - hurrying on
prestissimo - as fast as possible
presto - very quick
prima, primo - first
prima volta - first time

Q

quasi - as if, resembling

R

ralentir - slow down
rallentando [rall.] - becoming gradually slower
rapido, rapide, rasch - fast
religioso - religiously
repente - suddenly
retenu - held back
en retenant - holding back
ridicolosamente - humorously, inaccurate and loosely
rilassato - relaxed
rinforzando; [*rf*, *rfz*] - reinforcing
risoluto - boldly
ritardando [ritard., rit.] - gradually slower
ritenuto [riten., rit.] - hold back, slower at once
ritmico - rhythmically
rubato - flexible in tempo
ruhig - peaceful

S

sanft - gently
sans - without
scherzando, scherzoso -
     playfully, joking
scherzo - a joke
schnell - fast
schneller - faster
schwer - heavy
seconda, secondo - second

seconda volta - second time

segno - sign [𝄋]

    dal segno - from the sign, return to the point marked
        by segno

segue - go straight on

sehr - very

semplice - simple

sempre - always

sentito - expressively

senza - without

    senza sordini - without a mute

serioso - seriously

sforzando [*sf*, *sfz*] - with a sudden accent

simile [sim.] - in the same way

slancio - momentum

    con slancio - with momentum, with enthusiasm

slargando - becoming broader,
    becoming more largo

slentando - becoming slower,
    becoming more lento

smorzando [smorz.] - dying away

soave - smoothly, gently

somma - sum, total

    con somma passione - with great passion

sognando - dreamily

solenne - solemn

sonore - sonorous

sonoro - ringing, with rich
tone

sopra - above

soprano - the highest of the
    standard four voice
    ranges soprano, alto, tenor, bass

15

sospirando - sighing
sostenuto - sustained
sotto - below
> **sotto voce** - in an undertone

spianato - smooth, even
spirito - spirit
> **con spirito** – with spirit; with feeling

spiritoso - lively, animated
staccatissimo - very detached
staccato - short, detached
stentando - laboured, heavy, in a dragging manner,
  holding back each note
strepitoso - noisy, forceful
stringendo - gradually faster
subito - suddenly
sul G - play on the g string
sul ponticello - play near the bridge
suss - sweet

T

tacet - silent; do not play
tanto - so much
tempo - speed, time
> **a tempo** - resume the normal speed
>
> **a tempo** - in time; i.e., the performer should return to
>   the main tempo of the piece
>
> **tempo comodo** - at a comfortable speed
>
> **tempo di marcia** - march tempo
>
> **tempo di menuetto** - at the speed of a minuet
>
> **tempo di valse** - waltz tempo
>
> **tempo giusto** - in strict time
>
> **tempo primo** - resume the original speed

tempo rubato - with some freedom of time

teneramente, tenerezza - tenderly, tenderness

tenuto - held on

tenor - the second lowest of the
standard four voice ranges,
soprano, alto, tenor, bass

tosto - swift, rapid

tranquillo - calmly, peacefully

traurig - sad

très - very

triste, tristamente - sad, sorrowful

troppo - too much

allegro [ma] non troppo - fast but not too fast

tutti - all

U

un, une, uno, or una - one

und - and

V

veloce - speed/velocity

con veloce - with speed/velocity

velocissimo - as quickly as possible

vibrato - vibrating

vif; vite - lively, quick

vittorioso - victoriously

vivace, vivo - lively, quick

vivacissimo - very lively

voce - voice

volante - flying, fast

voll - full

volta - time

volti subito [v.s.] - turn the page quickly

W

wenig - little
wieder - again

Z

zart - tender, delicate
zartheit - tenderness
zärtlich - tenderly
zelo - zeal
zeloso - zealous
zelosamente - zealously
ziemlich - fairly, quite, rather
zu - to, too
zurückhalten - hold back

Signs & Symbols

LOOK UP
A SIGN

FIND THE MEANING

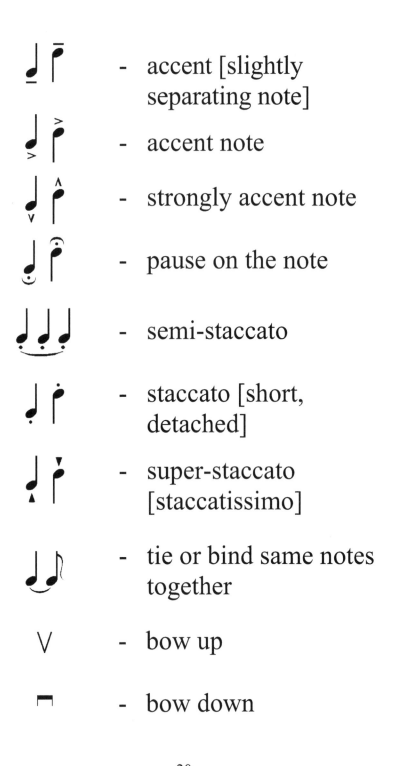

- accent [slightly separating note]

- accent note

- strongly accent note

- pause on the note

- semi-staccato

- staccato [short, detached]

- super-staccato [staccatissimo]

- tie or bind same notes together

- bow up

- bow down

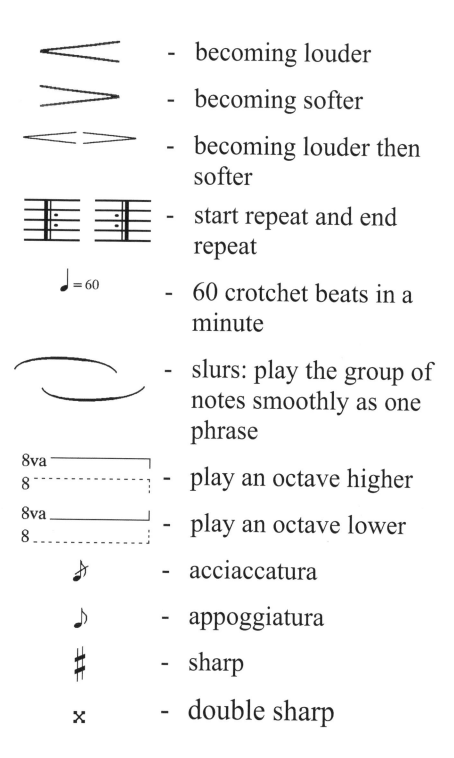

	-	becoming louder
	-	becoming softer
	-	becoming louder then softer
	-	start repeat and end repeat
♩ = 60	-	60 crotchet beats in a minute
	-	slurs: play the group of notes smoothly as one phrase
8va / 8	-	play an octave higher
8va / 8	-	play an octave lower
♪	-	acciaccatura
♪	-	appoggiatura
♯	-	sharp
x	-	double sharp

∾   -   turn

⅋   -   inverted turn

∿   -   upper mordent

∿   -   lower mordent

tr ∿∿∿   -   trill or shake

    -   arpeggio (harp-like)

Clefs

 Treble   Tenor

 Bass   Alto

Key Signatures (sharps)

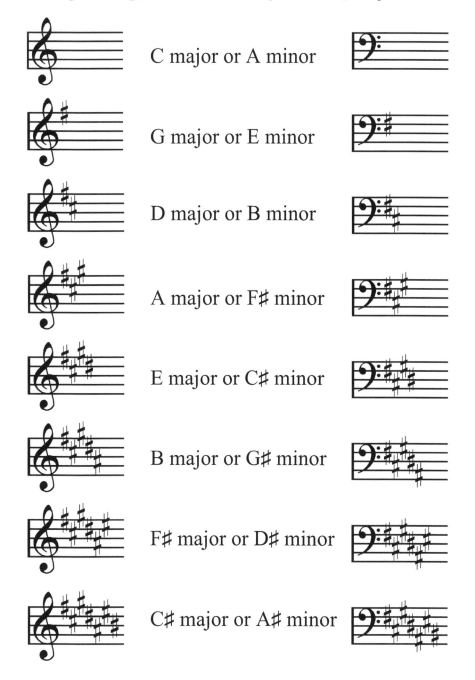

C major or A minor

G major or E minor

D major or B minor

A major or F♯ minor

E major or C♯ minor

B major or G♯ minor

F♯ major or D♯ minor

C♯ major or A♯ minor

Key Signatures (flats)

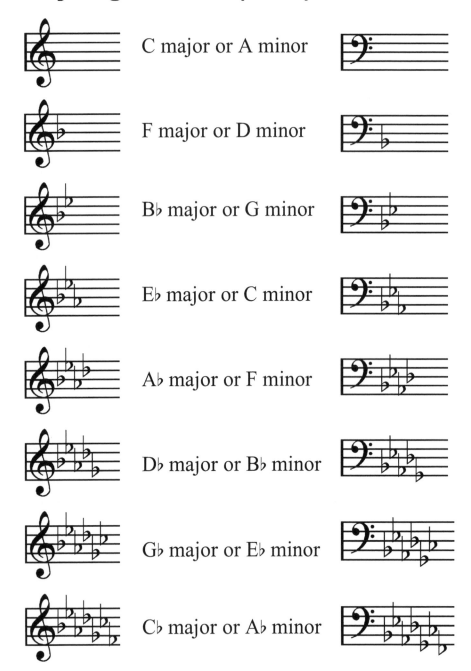

C major or A minor

F major or D minor

B♭ major or G minor

E♭ major or C minor

A♭ major or F minor

D♭ major or B♭ minor

G♭ major or E♭ minor

C♭ major or A♭ minor

Metronome & Tempo Guide

	Larghissimo
20	
	Grave
40	
	Largo
60	Lento
	Adagio
	Larghetto
80	Adagietto
	Andante
	Andantino
100	Andante moderato
	Moderato
	Allegretto
120	
	Allegro Moderato
	Allegro
140	
160	
	Vivace
	Allegro vivace
180	Vivacissimo
	Presto
200	
220	
	Prestissimo

Also by Maureen Cox

Theory is Fun Grade 1   **paperback**
ISBN 0 9516940 8 1

Treble clef, bass clef, notes and letter names. Time names and values. Dotted notes, tied notes and rests. Accidentals, tones and semitones. Key signatures and scales (C, G, D & F major). Degrees of the scale, intervals and tonic triads. Time signatures and bar-lines. Writing music and answering rhythms. Musical terms dictionary and list of signs.

Theory is Fun Grade 2   paperback
ISBN 1 898771 02 2

Major (A, Bb & Eb) and minor (A, E & D) key signatures and scales Degrees of the scale and intervals. Tonic triads. Piano keyboard, tones and semitones. Time signatures. Grouping notes and rests, triplets. Two ledger lines below and above the staves. Writing four-bar rhythms. More musical terms and signs.

Theory is Fun Grade 3   paperback
ISBN 1 898771 00 6

Major & minor key signatures 4 sharps or flats. Harmonic and melodic minor scales. Degrees of the scale, intervals, tonic triads. Simple and compound time signatures. Grouping notes & rests. Transposition at the octave. More than two ledger lines. Writing four-bar rhythms, anacrusis. Phrases and more musical terms & signs.

Theory is Fun Grade 4   paperback
ISBN 1 898771 01 4

All key signatures to 5 sharps or flats. Alto clef. Chromatic scale, double sharps & flats. Technical names of notes in the diatonic scale. Simple & compound time, duple, triple, quadruple. Primary triads, tonic, subdominant & dominant. All diatonic intervals up to an octave. Recognising ornaments. Four-bar rhythms and rhythms to words. Families of orchestral instruments and their clefs. More musical terms, including French

Theory is Fun Grade 5   paperback
ISBN 0 9516940 9 X

All key signatures to 7 sharps or flats. Tenor clef and scales. Compound intervals: major, minor, perfect, diminished and augmented. Irregular time signatures, quintuple & septuple. Tonic, supertonic, subdominant & dominant chords. Writing at concert pitch. Short & open score. Orchestral instruments in detail. Composing a melody for instrument or voice. Perfect, imperfect & plagal cadences. More musical terms, including German

Theory is Fun Grades 1 - 5 in a Nutshell　　　　　　　paperback
ISBN 1 898771 17 0
Major, relative harmonic & melodic minor keys. Chromatic scales.
Regular & irregular time signatures. Beaming & grouping of notes &
rests. Intervals, chords and cadences. Instruments of the orchestra.
Concert pitch & transposition. Short & open score. Composing a melody
for instrument or voice. Musical terms and signs.

Theory is Fun Activity Book 1　　　　　　　　　　　paperback
ISBN 1 898771 12 X
Letter names and notes in treble and bass clef. Time names and note
values. Dotted notes and rests. Key signatures and time signatures.
Degrees of the scale and intervals. Musical terms and signs. Introduction
to aural practice.

Theory is Fun in a Nutshell　　　　　　　　Kindle electronic book
ISBN 978 0 9866549 0 9
Major, relative harmonic & melodic minor keys. Chromatic scales.
Regular & irregular time signatures. Beaming & grouping of notes &
rests. Intervals, chords and cadences. Instruments of the orchestra.
Concert pitch & transposition. Short & open score. Composing a melody
for instrument or voice. Musical terms and signs.

Harmony is Fun Book 1　　　　　　　　　　　　　paperback
ISBN 1 898771 11 1
Common chords: tonic, dominant, subdominant　chords in close and
open position. Root position and first inversion. Chords spread between
treble and bass clef. Block and broken chords. The dominant 7th chord
and resolving. Perfect, imperfect and plagal cadence.

Harmony is Fun Book 2　　　　　　　　　　　　　paperback
ISBN 1 898771 14 6
Major & relative minor keys 3 sharps or flats. Supertonic, mediant and
submediant chords. Root position, first inversion, second inversion
chords spread between treble and bass clef. Open & closed block chords.
Broken chords. Substituting chords II, III & VI for IV, V & I . Resolving
- perfect and imperfect cadence.

Harmony is Fun Book 3　　　　　　　　　　　　　paperback
ISBN 1 898771 16 2
Major & relative minor keys 4 sharps or flats. Major & minor scales,
keys and chords in root position, first inversion, second inversion.
Dominant 7th chord and its third inversion. Biding notes. Melodic
decoration: essential & unessential notes - passing and auxiliary notes.
Modulation. Chord progression and fingering.

Blast Off with Music Theory Book 1   paperback
ISBN 1 56939 084 3
Treble clef and bass clef note names. Basic note values, including dotted notes, tied notes and rests. Accidentals, half and whole steps. Key signatures and major scales. Degrees of the scale, intervals and tonic triads. Basic time signatures. Basic rules of music writing. Music dictionary and list of signs.

Blast Off with Music Theory Book 2   paperback
ISBN 1 56939 085 1
Key signatures and major scales through 3 sharps and flats. Key signatures and minor scales through 1 sharp and flat. More about melodic and harmonic intervals. Sixteenth notes and rests, triplets. Tonic triads through 3 sharps and flats. Time signatures of 2/2 and 3/8. Grouping of notes when writing. More about ledger line notes. Music dictionary and list of signs.

Blast Off with Music Theory Book 3   paperback
ISBN 1 56939 086 X
Key signatures and major scales through 4 sharps and flats. Key signatures and minor scales through 2 sharps and 4 flats. Major and minor tonic triads. Simple and compound time signatures. Transposition. Note values, including dotted eighth notes. More ledger lines. Writing four-measure rhythms. The phrase. Music dictionary and list of signs.

Blast Off with Music Theory Book 4   paperback
ISBN 1 56939 087 8
Major and minor key signatures. Minor scales. Double sharps and flats. Scale degree names. Chromatic scales. Transposition by 2nds and 3rds. Simple & compound time signatures. Duplets and triplets. Thirty-second notes. Primary triads and inversions. Augmented and diminished intervals. Augmented and diminished triads. Common melodic ornaments. Music dictionary and music signs.

Blast Off with Music Theory Book 5   paperback
ISBN 1 56939 088 6
Major and minor key signatures. Circle of fifths. Major and minor scales. Pentatonic and whole-tone scales. Alto and tenor clefs. Instruments of the orchestra. Sixty-fourth notes and double-dotted note values. Irregular rhythmic figures. Irregular time signatures. Plagal, authentic and half cadences. Writing using music shorthand.

Musical Terms & Signs in a Nutshell   Kindle electronic book
ISBN 978 0 9866549 7 8
A dictionary and a handy chart of all the major and minor key signatures.

Books and Music published by Mimast Inc

available from Music Exchange (Manchester) Ltd
www.music-exchange.co.uk

Printed Books	ISBN
Theory is Fun - Grade 1	0 9516940 8 1
Theory is Fun - Activity Book 1	1 898771 12 X
Theory is Fun - Grade 2	1 898771 02 2
Theory is Fun - Grade 3	1 898771 00 6
Theory is Fun - Grade 4	1 898771 01 4
Theory is Fun - Grade 5	0 9516940 9 X
Music Theory Grades 1-5 In A Nutshell	1 898771 17 0
Musical Terms Word Search In A Nutshell	9781987926057
Harmony is Fun - Book 1	0 9516940 0 6
Harmony is Fun - Book 2	1 898771 14 6
Harmony is Fun - Book 3	1 898771 16 2

Printer Music	ISBN
Upbeat for Piano - Level 0	1 898771 09 X
Upbeat for Piano - Level 1	1 898771 04 9
Upbeat for Piano - Level 2	1 898771 05 7
Upbeat for Piano - Level 3	1 898771 06 5
Upbeat for Piano - Level 4	1 898771 07 3
Upbeat for Piano - Level 5	1 898771 08 1
Upbeat! For Clarinet Book 1	1 898771 18 9
Upbeat! For Flute or Oboe Book 1	1 898771 19 7
Upbeat! For Saxophone Book 1	1 898771 22 7
Upbeat! For Violin Book 1	1 898771 20 0
Upbeat! For Violin Book 2	1 898771 21 9
Upbeat for Small Jazz Groups	1 898771 15 4

available from Amazon
www.amazon.com and www.amazon.co.uk

Printed Books	ISBN
Musical Terms Word Search In A Nutshell	9780986654992

Kindle Electronic Books	ISBN
Music Theory In A Nutshell	9780986654909
Musical Terms & Signs In A Nutshell	9780986654978

Printed in Great Britain
by Amazon